ANNIE

A CHARACTER SKETCH

1891

BY

W. T. STEAD

Editor of *The Review of Reviews*

THE THEOSOPHICAL PUBLISHING HOUSE
ADYAR, MADRAS, INDIA
1946

The Theosophical Publishing House desires to express its thanks to the Editor of *The Review of Reviews* for permission to reprint this " Character Sketch of Annie Besant " by W. T. Stead.

Printed by C. Subbarayudu, at the Vasanta Press,
The Theosophical Society, Adyar, Madras,
P.I.C. No. 85—21-12-46

MOTHER AND DAUGHTER : 1867

FOREWORD

THE public life of England has produced many champions of the people, but none who in his time was more valiant than W. T. Stead. In his journalistic life he was best known as the editor of the *Pall Mall Gazette* published in the afternoons in London. The paper, which had had John Morley for editor, under Mr. Stead as editor was widely read in all parts of Britain, because it stood not merely for Liberalism in politics, but was also the champion of all schemes for the liberalisation of the thoughts and minds of the British people. He introduced what is now commonplace in journalism—the interview.

Mr. Stead was built in a heroic mould, so that he was not deterred by the laws of the country in writing openly concerning the commercial exploitation of prostitution, which was known to but was tolerated by the police. He was condemned for his action (the legal reasons do not matter now) for three months in Holloway Goal. A book which he wrote concerning the underworld of Chicago, *If Christ came to Chicago*, equally showed his fiery indignation against the tolerance of degrading evils in civic life.

An innovation in journalism was *The Review of Reviews*, which summarised briefly all the reviews that appeared in any country in the course of the month. But in addition there were observations by Mr. Stead, brief editorials concerning what was happening in the political and social field, that were read first by the reader. The *Review of Reviews* became one of the great magazines of Britain. It still continues.

The strong link between Annie Besant and W. T. Stead is thus described by her in her book *Annie Besant—An Autobiography* : [1]

> Out of all this turmoil and stress rose a Brotherhood that had in it the promise of a fairer day. Mr. Stead and I had become close friends—he Christian, I Atheist, burning with one common love for man, one common hatred against oppression. And so in *Our Corner* for February, 1888, I wrote :
>
> "Lately there has been dawning on the minds of men far apart in questions of theology, the idea of founding a new Brotherhood, in which service of Man should take the place erstwhile given to service of God

[1] London Edition, 1917.

—a brotherhood in which work should be worship and love should be baptism, in which none should be regarded as alien who was willing to work for human good. One day as I was walking towards Millbank Gaol with the Rev. S. D. Headlam, on the way to liberate a prisoner, I said to him : 'Mr. Headlam, we ought to have a new Church, which should include all who have the common ground of faith in and love for man.' And a little later I found that my friend Mr. W. T. Stead, editor of the *Pall Mall Gazette*, had long been brooding over a similar thought, and wondering whether men 'might not be persuaded to be as earnest about making this world happy as they were over saving their souls'. . . As a step towards bringing about some such union of those ready to work for man, Mr. Stead and I projected the *Link*, a halfpenny weekly, the spirit of which was described in its motto, taken from Victor Hugo 'The people are silence. I will be the advocate of this silence. I will speak for the dumb. I will speak of the small to the great and of the feeble to the strong. . . .' Week after week we issued our little paper, and it became a real light in the darkness." (pp. 329—331).

Of greater and more far-reaching consequence to Annie Besant was that it was Mr. Stead who threw open to her the door to her greatest career, which was as a Theosophist. She thus describes what happened :

At last, sitting alone in deep thought as I had become accustomed to do after the sun had set, filled with an intense but nearly hopeless longing to solve the riddle of life and mind, I heard a Voice that was later to become to me the holiest sound on earth, bidding me take courage for the light was near. A fortnight passed, and then Mr. Stead gave into my hands two large volumes. "Can you review these? My young men all fight shy of them, but you are quite mad enough on these subjects to make something of them." I took the books; they were the two volumes of *The Secret Doctrine*, written by H. P. Blavatsky. . . . I wrote the review, and asked Mr. Stead for an introduction to the writer, and then sent a note asking to be allowed to call. I received the most cordial of notes, bidding me come. (pp. 340—1).

The *Character Sketch* which I have asked the Theosophical Publishing House to reprint is one which I have never forgotten from the time it appeared. To all of us who knew Annie Besant, it brings her character back to us vividly, and indicates too some of the greater actions which she was yet to do after she entered the Theosophical Society and, in the course of time, became one of the leaders of the Indian National Movement.

Mr. Stead was one of hundreds who lost their lives on April 15, 1912, when S. S. *Titanic*, then the largest steamer, speeded across the Atlantic on her first voyage and in a fog collided with an iceberg. Mr. Stead from 1893 to 1897 published *Borderland*, a paper dealing with all facts concerning spiritualism, telepathy, etc., that linked the visible world with the invisible. After his death some communications were received through spiritualistic séances which were satisfactory to those who knew him as being from the real W. T. Stead, and not from some impersonator on the other side of the veil.

Mr. Stead's *Life* has been published by his daughter, Miss Estelle Stead.

C. JINARÂJADÂSA

CONTENTS

W. T. STEAD

CHARACTER SKETCH

BY W. T. STEAD

ONE of the most difficult things in writing these sketches is the attempt to delineate the character of one's personal friends. It is easier to do it if your friend has passed into the realm where the *Review* does not circulate, but it is always difficult, and sometimes impossible. There are so many things that you would like to say that you cannot say ; yet, if you do not say them, you cannot quite explain why you think as you do about your friend. A great deal must be left unsaid ; and thus, although you may express the conclusions at which you have arrived, it is next to impossible for you to justify them to the satisfaction of those who only know what the writer prints, which is necessarily only a small—a very small—part of the intimate knowledge on which his opinion is based. Mrs. Besant's case is a typical instance of this difficulty. I admit at the outset it is insuperable, and content myself with pleading that even those who may most dissent from my judgment might reverse their opinion if they could but really be admitted to a confidence which is impossible in a publication addressed to all the world.

Annie Besant is now, as she has been for the last four or five years, one of my most intimate friends. I had not the privilege of knowing her in her earliest phase, either of school-girl Evangelicalism or of young-woman Puseyism, but I knew her as Materialist and Atheist. I know her as Theosophist, and whatever development she may pass through will in no way affect the sentiment of affectionate admiration with which I regard her. She is one of the three remarkable women of the apostolic type of this generation. Mrs. Booth, Mrs. Butler, and Mrs. Besant constitute a remarkable trio of propagandists militant, whose zeal, energy, and enthusiasm have left a deep impress upon our time. Of the three, Mrs. Besant is the youngest, having been born in 1847 ; and as she is not yet five-and-forty, she may live to take her seat, together with Mrs. Fawcett, in the House of Commons. Mrs. Booth is no longer with us. Mrs. Butler, although a widow, stricken in years and afflicted, still tends the sacred fire which she has kindled in the hearts of men. But Mrs. Besant is the only one of the three who is still in her prime, whose last words have not yet been spoken, and whose ultimate development is still unknown. Last month her name was in every mouth, and the papers were filled with endless letters discussing the latest phase of her progress in search of truth. Next month she is to start for India, not only as a pilgrim from the West to the shrines sacred to the wisdom of the East, but as a missionary and propagandist of the faith which had Madame Blavatsky as its most conspicuous seer. The other day she was presiding over a Socialist Congress in Paris, next year no one can say where she will be or what she will be doing, except that, whatever she may do or wherever she may go, one thing only is quite certain, she will be animated by a passionate love and sympathy for the poor and oppressed, and she will command the enthusiastic affection of all those who come near enough to her to know her as she really is.

Yet Mrs. Besant, one of the half-dozen women who have stamped the impress of their strong and vivid personality upon their own time, is one to whom, until but the other day, it was considered hardly correct to allude, except in the most distant manner, as if she inhabited another and improper world. When I started this *Review* I had to put my foot down, before the first number saw the light, on an attempt to enforce even in these pages the policy of boycott that still prevails in certain obscure quarters. Mrs. Besant had written me a cordial little note welcoming the new *Review*, which was inserted among the other letters which I received from the eminent men and women of the day. The business side of the *Review* remonstrated. "Was very sorry, you know, really. Great regard for Mrs. Besant, but business is business, and it would never do, and especially in the first number, to parade her name. Couldn't Mr. Stead leave it over till February?" To which the editorial side replied as might be expected, only to elicit the further protest: "Well, of course, if you will, you must, but remember, that name will cost us hundreds of subscribers. There are scores of clergymen who will never allow the *Review* to enter their doors if Mrs. Besant's name appears in its columns." That may or may not be true. If it is, so much the worse for the clergymen in question. Of course her letter went in. But the protest was interesting as illustrating the kind of prejudice which has existed about Mrs. Besant.

It may be that even now some readers may have so little entered into the spirit with which every page of this magazine has been written since that first summary over-ruling of the protests against the publication of her letter, as to object to the selection of Mrs. Besant as the subject of this Character Sketch. All that I need say to them is, whether they be many or few, that when they have made a tithe of her sacrifices for conscience' sake they may be in a position to criticise. Until then they will do well to be silent, and endeavour, if they can, to catch a little of her spirit. Most of those who sneer at her as if she were disreputable, or shrug their shoulders when her name is mentioned, might then perhaps come to be numbered among those who are worthy to unloose the latchet of her shoe.

One result of the persistent boycott that has been maintained against her so long by the papers is that one of the most charming and pathetic autobiographical sketches in our language is practically non-existent for the great mass of the English-speaking public. Mrs. Besant's fragmentary sketches of her spiritual pilgrimage, although published in 1885, is, I suppose, almost unknown to my readers. The book is out of print, and they will therefore be grateful for the extracts which I shall make freely from its pages. I hope, now the ice has been broken, and the great slow-minded public has wakened up at last to the fact that Mrs. Besant is one of the most remarkable women of our time, she will republish it, with an additional chapter describing the later stages of her pilgrim's progress. An authentic narrative of the soul-journeyings of an intensely religious soul from Evangelicalism to Puseyism, and thence through Broad Church Theism to the flat negations of an Atheistic Materialism, out of which she has emerged, by way of Spiritualism, into the realm of Theosophy, is one for which we may search in vain in contemporary religious biography. Such a story could not fail to be full of suggestion in any case, even if the writer were obscure and unknown. How much more interesting, then, must it be when it reaches us from one of the most eloquent of living women, who is still in the zenith of her powers.

I. HEREDITY AND EDUCATION

ANNIE BESANT is Besant only by marriage, Her husband, the Rev. Frank Besant, vicar of Sibsey, in Lincolnshire, is a brother of Mr. Walter Besant, the well-known novelist. Her maiden name was Wood. She is a Wood of the family which gave us a Lord Chancellor in the person of Lord Hatherley, and many others who have played a more or less notable part in our local and national politics. One of the clan is said to have obtained a baronetcy as a reward for enabling Queen Victoria to be born in England. He was Lord Mayor, and a man of substance. Of that substance, he parted freely to pay the Duke of Kent's debts, in order that the heir to the English throne might be born on English soil.

HER FATHER

Her father, who was Lord Hatherley's cousin, belonged to the elder branch, which had clung to the estate in Devonshire, from which the younger sons had gone off to make fortunes in business and at the bar. He was born and educated in Ireland, where he took his degree as a doctor, although he seldom practised. He held a good appointment in the City of London, and seems to have been a man of considerable parts. His daughter says of him :

> A mathematician and a good classic scholar, thoroughly master of French, German, Italian, Spanish, and Portuguese, with a smattering of Hebrew and Gaelic, the treasures of ancient and modern literature were his household delight. Student of philosophy as he was, he was deeply and steadily sceptical. His mother and sister were strict Roman Catholics, and near the end forced a priest into his room, but the priest was promptly ejected by the wrath of the dying man.

An Ideal Mother

Mrs. Besant's mother was Irish—one of the Morrises, who boast of their descent from some fabulous Milesian kings who hailed from France. When her mother was a child, the regular form of reproof when she had misbehaved was : " Emily, your conduct is unworthy of the descendants of the Seven Kings of France "—a curious form of that spur and curb chain which Lord Wolseley told us last month was to be found in the consciousness of noble birth. Mrs. Besant knew little of her father, for she was but five years old when he died, but she idolised her mother. She says :

> The tenderest, sweetest, proudest, noblest woman I have ever known. I have never met a woman more selflessly devoted to those she loved, more passionately contemptuous of all that was mean and base, more keenly sensitive on every question of honour, more iron in will, more sweet in tenderness, than the mother who made my girlhood sunny as dreamland, who guarded me until my marriage from every touch of pain that she could ward off.
>
> She never allowed a trouble of any kind to touch me, and cared only that all the worries should fall on her and the joys on me. No hand but hers must dress my hair, which loosed, fell in dense curly masses nearly to my knees ; no hand but hers must fasten dresses and deck with flowers. So guarded and shielded had been my childhood and youth from every touch of pain and anxiety that love could bear for me, that I never dreamed that life might be a heavy burden, save as I saw it in the poor I was sent to help. All the joy of those happy years I took, not ungratefully, I hope, but certainly with a glad unconsciousness of anything rare in it, as I took the sunlight.

The home seems to have been for these first five years almost ideally happy. But when the blow fell, and Mr. Wood died in October 1852, the light of life seemed for a time to have gone out. The agony of the bereavement blanched her mother's raven locks as white as snow in a single night.

A Case of Psychical Heredity

The first glimpse we have into the peculiar psychical temperament which has impelled Mrs. Besant to join the Theosophists occurs in an anecdote she tells about her mother in connection with the death of her father. The clairvoyant faculty that is implied in the following narrative has probably had as much to do as anything with recent developments.

I sat in an upstairs room with my mother and her sisters; and still comes back to me her figure seated on a sofa, with fixed white face and dull vacant eyes, counting the minutes until the funeral procession would have reached Kensal Green, and then following in mechanical fashion, Prayer-book in hand, the service, stage by stage, until to my unspeakable terror, with the words dully spoken, "It is all over," she fell back fainting. And here comes a curious psychological problem which has often puzzled me. Some weeks later she resolved to go and see her husband's grave. A relative who had been present at the funeral volunteered to guide her to the spot, but lost his way in that wilderness of graves. Another of the small party went off to find one of the officials, and to inquire, and my mother said: "If you will take me to the chapel where the first part of the service was read I will find the grave." To humour her whim he led her thither, and looking round for a moment or two she started from the chapel, followed the path along which the coffin had been borne, and was standing by the newly-made grave when the official came to point it out. Her own explanation is that she had seen all the service; what is certain is, that she never had been to Kensal Green before, and that she walked steadily from the chapel to the grave. She must have been, of course, at that time in a state of abnormal nervous excitation, a state of which another proof was shortly afterwards given. The youngest of our family was a boy, about three years younger than myself, a very beautiful child, blue-eyed and golden-haired—I have still a lock of his hair, of exquisite pale golden hue—and the little lad was passionately devoted to his father. He was always a delicate boy, and had, I suppose, therefore, been specially petted, and he fretted continually for "papa." It is probable that the consumptive taint had touched him, for he pined steadily away with no marked disease during the winter months. One morning my mother calmly stated, "Alf is going to die." It was in vain that it was urged on her that with spring strength would return to the child. "No," she persisted, "he was lying asleep in my arms last night, and William came and said he wanted Alf with him, but that I might keep the other two." She had in her a strong strain of Celtic superstition, and thoroughly believed that this vision—a most natural dream under the circumstances—was a direct "warning," and that her husband had come to tell her of her approaching loss. This belief was fully justified by the little fellow's death in the following March, calling to the end for "Papa! Papa!"

That "strong strain of Celtic superstition" would probably be differently described by the successor of Madame Blavatsky.

Dean Vaughan and the Widowed Family

Mrs. Wood's was much too strong a nature to remain prostrate even under a blow whose force was attested by the blanching of her hair. Left a widow, with a young family and next to no means, she never flinched, but set about carrying out the dying wish of her husband that their eldest boy should have the best possible education.

It seemed madness for a penniless widow to persist in sending her boy to Harrow School in

DEAN VAUGHAN

order to prepare him for a University career, but she stuck to it and ultimately carried it through. That she was able to do this was largely due to the kind support of Dr. Vaughan, now Master of the Temple, who was then Headmaster of Harrow. He allowed her to take some of the Harrow boys into her own house—a rambling, rose and ivy covered building on the very summit of Harrow Hill—and by this means she was able not only to keep herself, but to find means for the education of her son. Dr. Vaughan, Mrs. Besant gratefully remarks, became the earnest friend and helper of her mother, and to the counsel and active assistance both of himself and of his wife was due much of the success that crowned her toil. This house—the old vicarage at Harrow—was her home for eleven years—a place of idyllic joy, contrasting strongly with the stormy and troubled career that followed after.

Her Childhood at Harrow

Little Annie for a short time was brought up among the boys—as good a cricketer and climber as any of them, but so passionately devoted to her mother, that when being teased once about her clinging affection, " I will tie you to my apron with a string," the little one replied, " Oh, mamma, darling, do let it be in a knot ! " She revelled in the freedom and beauty of the spacious garden and its bees and flowers, and its far-extended outlook over one of the loveliest of English landscapes.

> There was not a tree there that I did not climb, and one, a widespreading Portugal laurel, was my private country-house. I had there my bedroom and my sitting-rooms, my study and my larder. The larder was supplied by the fruit trees, from which I was free to pick as I would, and in the study I would sit for hours with some favourite book —Milton's *Paradise Lost* the chief favourite of all. I liked to personify Satan, and declaim the grand speeches of the hero-rebel, and many a happy hour did I pass in Milton's heaven and hell, with for companions Satan and " the Son," Gabriel and Abdiel.

Educated by Capt. Marryat's Sister

After a short time, however, these delights were only for the holidays. Miss Marryat, the favourite sister of Captain Marryat, a lame lady with a strong face and as strong a character, undertook her education. It was Miss Marryat's method of making herself useful in the world. She had a perfect genius for teaching, and having undertaken to educate a niece, soon discovered that education would progress better if her scholar had a companion. Mrs. Besant's meeting with her was merely by chance. She took to the child and offered to educate her free of charge. After a brief struggle mother and child parted, and little Annie passed over to the household of Miss Marryat. It was a very fortunate arrangement. "No words can tell," Mrs. Besant wrote in after years, "how much I owe her, not only of knowledge, but of that love of knowledge which has remained with me ever since as a constant spur to study." Other children, "gently born and gently trained," were from time to time added to the party, for Miss Marryat was a lady of independent fortune, to whom it was a joy to spend her means in helping on their way gentle folk in difficulties.

Mrs. Besant's account of her education shows that her new "Auntie" was a woman of common sense, independent of conventionality. Boys and girls were alike taught to sew ; the only grammar used was the Latin, spelling books were superseded by constant familar letters or essays, written by the children and corrected in class, and geography by skeleton maps and puzzle maps. French and German were taught thoroughly, and finished afterwards in Paris and on the Rhine. Plenty of exercise, long walks, pony rides, and other delights of country life in a charming Devonshire village, kept the children healthy and happy. "Never was a healthier home, physically and mentally, made for young things than in that quiet village."

Her Evangelical Training

Miss Marryat was a rigid Evangelical, whose earnest creed naturally exercised a lasting influence upon the enthusiastic girl she had undertaken to teach. The hero of *Pilgrim's Progress* succeeded Milton's fallen Archangel as the ideal of her devotion. Always militant, she regretted that Christians did not do tangible battle, armed cap-à-pie, with Appollyon and Giant Despair, instead of being called merely to learn lessons, keep one's temper, and mend one's stockings. But "Auntie's" religion, although orthodox, was always hitched on to the practical duties of daily life. It is easy to see the germ of much of present-day Socialism in the teachings of the Evangelical preceptress.

She visited the poor, taking help wherever she went, and sending food from her own table to the sick. It was characteristic that she would never give " scraps " to the poor, but would have a basin brought in at dinner and cut the best slice to tempt the invalid appetite. Money, if ever, she rarely gave, but she would find a day's work or busy herself to find permanent employment for any one asking aid. Stern in rectitude herself, and iron to the fawning or dishonest, her influene, whether she was feared or loved, was always for good. Of the strictest sect of the Evangelicals she was an Evangelical. On Sundays no book was allowed but the Bible or the *Sunday at Home* ; but she would try to make the days bright by various little devices : by a walk with her in the garden, by the singing of hymns, always attractive to children, by telling us wonderful missionary stories of Moffat and Livingstone, whose adventures with savages and wild beasts were as exciting as any tale of Mayne Reid's. We used to learn passages from the Bible and hymns for repetition ; a favourite amusement was a " Bible puzzle," such as a description of a Bible scene which was to be recognised by the description. Then we taught in the Sunday-School, for Auntie would tell us it was useless to learn if we did not try to teach those who had no one to teach them. The

2

Sunday-School lessons had to be carefully prepared on Saturday, for we were always taught that work done for the poor should always be work that cost something to the giver. This principle, regarded by her as an illustration of the text " Shall I give unto the Lord my God that which has cost me nothing ? " ran through all her precept and practice.

Confirmed

The sensitive, dreamy, enthusiastic child was made to take part in the school prayer meeting, taught to eschew theatres, to regard balls as an abomination, and generally to walk in the straight and narrow way. During seven happy workful months spent in Paris, she was confirmed in an ecstasy of excitement. " I could scarcely control myself as I knelt at the altar rails, and felt as though the gentle touch of the aged Bishop, which fluttered for an instant on my bowed head, was the very touch of the wing of that Holy Spirit, heavenly Dove, whose presence had been so earnestly invoked."

After returning to England, Mrs. Besant prosecuted her French and German studies, and cultivated music with a passion that appears to have been inherited from her mother.

HER EARLY READING

After leaving Miss Marryat's care, the young girl, in the less austere atmosphere of Harrow, relaxed the severity of her views as to the amusements of the world. She was devoted to archery and croquet, and danced to her heart's content with the junior masters, "who could talk as well as flirt." Never had a girl a happier home life.

The atmosphere surrounding me was literary rather than scientific. I remember reading a translation of Plato that gave me great delight, and being rather annoyed by the insatiable questionings of Socrates. Lord Derby's translation of the Iliad also charmed me with its stateliness and melody, and Dante was another favourite study. Wordsworth and Cowper I much disliked, and into the same category went all the seventeenth and eighteenth century "poets," though I read them conscientiously through. Southey fascinated me with his wealth of Oriental fancies, while Spenser was a favourite book put beside Milton and Dante. My novel reading was extremely limited : indeed the three-volume novel was a forbidden fruit. My mother regarded these ordinary love stories as unhealthy reading for a young girl, and gave me Scott and Kingsley, but not Miss Braddon and Mrs. Henry Wood. Nor would she take me to the theatre, though we went to really good concerts. She had a horror of sentimentality in girls, and loved to see them bright and gay and above all, absolutely ignorant of all evil things and of premature love dreams. Happy, healthy, and workful were those too brief years.

The Library of the Fathers

About this time Mrs. Besant came upon the books which brought about the first of the many notable changes in her theological views which form so marked a feature in her life. On the bookshelves of the old vicarage at Harrow she found "The Library of the Fathers," and began to read.

Soon those strange mystic writers won over me a great fascination, and I threw myself ardently into the question: "Where is now the Catholic Church?" I read Pusey and Liddon and Keble, with many another of that school and many of the seventeenth century English divines. I began to fast—to the intense disapproval of my mother, who cared for her health far more than for all the Fathers the Church could boast of—to use the sign of the cross, and go to weekly communion. Indeed, the contrast I found between my early Evangelical training and the doctrines of the primitive Christian Church would have driven me over to Rome had it not been for the proofs afforded by Pusey and his co-workers that the English Church might be

Catholic although non-Roman. But for them I should certainly have joined the Papal Communion; for if the Church of the early centuries be compared with that of Rome and Geneva, there is no doubt that Rome shows marks of primitive Christianity of which Geneva is entirely devoid.

Her High Church Phase

What might have happened if the half-way house of Anglicanism had not arrested the impulse Romewards, suggests some interesting speculations. Would the most immobile of Churches have been able to fix the faith of this most mobile of creatures, who has indeed plenty of *vim*, but to whom the saving solid security of the *vis inertiae* seems to have been entirely denied?

It was the day of the High Church Revival, and Mrs. Besant—like many another young girl who had not read the Fathers—found much solace for her soul's need in making ornaments and arranging decorations for the Mission Chapel near Albert Square, Clapham Road. In this also resembling her less erudite sisters, her ecclesiastical zeal led her to make the acquaintance of a young cleric, the Rev. Frank Besant, a

Cambridge man, who helped at the Mission, and kept himself as under-master of Stockwell Grammar School.

Her First Doubt

It was while still in the heyday of her Anglican enthusiasm that Mrs. Besant was first startled by the shadow of the approaching eclipse of faith. She was a vehement Irish girl, who looked at heretics and heresy through the spectacles of the early Christian Fathers. The possibility of doubting seemed to her at once as remote and as loathsome as the possibility of being infected with leprosy, when suddenly across her mind fell the darkness of sudden doubt. In Holy Week, 1866, she set herself to construct a harmony of the four Gospels concerning the events of the Passion. She soon discovered, apparently for the first time in her life, that there were discrepancies between the Evangelical records. She threw down her pen and shut the Bible. Then she shrank back penitent and horror-stricken before this yielding to the temptation of the devil. She fasted as a penance for her involuntary sin of unbelief, and trampling down the doubt with Tertullian's *Credo quia impossibile*, she accepted the apparent inconsistency as a thing to be believed blindly as of faith, and not to be too closely examined into by the reason. "The awful threat, 'He that believeth not shall be damned,' sounded in my ears, and like the angel with the flaming sword. barred the path of all too curious inquiry." She was not yet through her twentieth year, and had already been Evangelical, worldly, and High Church, and now, for the first time, the Demon of Doubt had asked its poisonous question and marked her for his own.

II. HER MARRIED LIFE

TWO years before Mrs. Besant attained her majority, she was in the mood, which is more common than is generally supposed, due to the diversion of a woman's thoughts from an earthly to a heavenly Bridegroom. If she had been a Catholic, she would have become a nun and spent the rest of her days in ecstatic devotion, finding all the consolation that worldly women find in husband and lover in the mystic figure of the Crucified. As she was an Anglican, she married a curate. She had no love dreams, she had "read no fiery novels," and had lived a healthy active life. She says :

> I longed to spend my time in worshipping Jesus, and was, as far as my inner life was concerned, absorbed in that passionate love of the Saviour which among emotional Catholics really is the human passion of love transferred to an ideal—for women to Jesus, for men to the Virgin Mary.

Her prayers at this period were like those of ecstatic nuns, full of the passion of the bride in

HOW TO BECOME A MAHATMA!

The Evolution of Mrs. Besant

(From the *St. Stephen's Review,* 12 Sept. 1891.)

the Song of Solomon. It is the usual outlet which religion supplies for the dawning feelings of womanhood, which are, as she remarks, as certain to be the more intense and earnest as the nature is deep and loving.

Her Mother's One Mistake

Her mother was revolted at this phase of religious emotion. She had kept her daughter ignorantly innocent of the nature of men and women, through the customary conventional delusion that ignorance is the same as innocence. It was then, as always, a blunder, and in her case a fatal blunder. She became engaged to the young clergyman, not because she loved him particularly, or had even the faintest conception of what marriage entailed, but only because it seemed as if he, being a clergyman, could, by his very office, bring her nearer to God. The position of a clergyman's wife, she remarks, seems second only to that of a nun, and its attractiveness had very little to do with the personality of the particular clergyman who is selected to discharge the sacred functions.

Her Marriage

When she consented to marry Mr. Besant, she gave up with a sigh of regret her dreams of the religious life, and substituted for them the work which would have to be done as the wife of a parish priest, labouring in the Church and among the poor. She reluctantly consented to marry a man she did not much care for, because she believed him, by virtue of his office, a half-angelic creature, and, to her, wedlock was only a means of self-devotion to the cause of the poor and the service of the Church. No doubt it seems almost incredible to those who do not know women, and the immense capacity which blank ignorance has of ignoring facts, that a woman as intelligent, as healthy and as keen, as Mrs. Besant could have left her home a bride as absolutely unaware of what marriage meant as a babe of four ; but it is unfortúnately by no means an isolated phenomenon. To the criminal wickedness of parents in this respect there seems sometimes to be literally no limit. A little elementary physiology would have stood her in better stead than "The Library of the Fathers." But she read the Fathers, who told her much of the world to come, while no one told her anything about the world in which she was living, and the duties and responsibilities of a wife. Hence, when, in December 1867, her betrothed took her to the steps of the altar and they became husband and wife, it was as if the illusions of life had vanished.

Her Initiation into Politics

Just before her marriage Miss Wood made her first acquaintance with the regions of political storm and stress in which she was hereafter to swell. The merry school-girl had but little thought for the affairs of the hustings, and all that she knew, or thought she knew, about John Bright, for instance, was that "he was a rough sort of man who goes about making rows." Mr. Roberts, the Radical lawyer of Manchester, rudely roused her from that state of apathy by declaring his belief that "some of you fine ladies would not go to heaven if you had to rub shoulders with John Bright, the noblest man God ever gave to the cause of the poor." It was by this Mr. Roberts that she was first initiated into Radicalism, and it was when she was on a visit at his house in Manchester that she first actually participated as a spectator in one of those stormy and tragic interludes of politics in which she has subsequently passed so much of her life. Mr. Roberts was the solicitor for the Irishmen who were tried and hanged at Manchester for the murder of Sergeant Brett. The Irish national anthem, "God Save Ireland," owes its inspiration to the execution that followed that trial. Mrs. Besant first caught in the crowded court where that judicial blunder was legalised a sense of the infinite tragedy and ruthless crime that lurk behind the political struggles of our time.

Her Husband

It is not necessary to say much about the Rev. Frank Besant. He had a trying part to fill, and it may be permissible to say that he was hardly equal to the task. He was a clergyman, conventional and conservative. He had brought home a wild young thing whose heart was aflame with the first passion of political sympathy with the Irish and the Radicals, and who had only married him as a *pis aller*. She could not be the Bride of Heaven, and therefore became the bride of Mr. Frank Besant. He was hardly an adequate substitute. Mr. Besant had obtained a master-ship at Cheltenham, and there in lodgings his young wife tried to stifle the cruel sense of disillusion by hard reading and, curiously enough, by writing stories for the *Family Herald*, for which she received her first earned money, and a series of "Lives of the Black Letter Saints," which, however, failed to find a publisher. Then she published her first pamphlet, a little tract which insisted upon the virtue of fasting and was very patristic in tone.

For Baby's Sake

Two children were born, first a boy and then a girl. The latter was seven months old when she became the unconscious instrument in waking the stifled doubts of her mother. It was from a baby's cradle that the impulse came which drove Mrs. Besant from the Christian fold. Little Mabel Besant, like other infants, had the whooping cough, and had it so bad that her life was despaired of, and more than once she was believed to have actually died. Thanks, however, to her mother's tender care, the child survived. But its mother's faith was rudely shattered. She tells us that during these silent weeks that she sat with a dying child on her knees, watching for death, until she collapsed from sheer exhaustion, the important change of mind took place.

There had grown up in my mind a feeling of angry resentment against the God who had been for weeks, as I thought, torturing my helpless baby. For some months a stubborn antagonism to the Providence who ordains the sufferings of life had steadily been increasing in me, and this sullen challenge, "Is God good ?" found voice in my heart during these silent nights and days. My mother's sufferings and much personal unhappiness had been intensifying the feeling, and as I watched my baby in its agony, and felt so helpless to relieve, more than once the indignant cry broke from my lips : "How canst Thou torture a baby so ? What has she done that she should suffer so ? Why dost Thou not kill her at once and let her be at peace ?" More than once I cried aloud, "Oh God, take the child, but do not torment her." All my personal belief in God, all my intense faith in His constant direction of affairs, all my habit of continual prayer and of realisation of His presence, were now against me. To me He was not an abstract idea, but a living reality, and all my mother-heart rose up in rebellion against this Person in whom I believed, and whose individual finger I saw in my baby's agony.

THE STRUGGLE TO BELIEVE

Then ensued weeks and months of agonised battling against the doubt which threatened to transform the Almighty Father into an almighty fiend. A good and liberal clergyman gave her kindly counsel, lent her Maurice and Robertson to read, and strove, but strove in vain, to lead her into their wider hope for man, their more trustful faith in God. She was in mental agony as real as the pain which tortured her child, and she would find no rest.

The thought of hell was torturing me. Somehow, out of the baby's pain, through those seemingly endless hours, had grown a dim realisation of what hell might be, full of the sufferings of the beloved ; and my whole brain and heart revolted from the unutterable cruelty of a creating and destroying God. . . . The presence of evil and pain in the world made by a "good God," and the pain falling on the innocent, as in my seven-months-old babe, the pain here reaching on into eternity unhealed ; these, while I yet believed, drove me desperate, and I believed and hated instead of, like the devils, "believed and trembled." Next, I challenged the righteousness of the doctrine of the Atonement, and while I worshipped and clung to the suffering Christ, I hated the God who required the death-sacrifice at His hands. And so for months the turmoil went on, the struggle being all the more terrible for the very desperation with which I strove to cling to some planks of the wrecked ship of faith on the tossing sea of doubt.

The Agony of Doubt

No one who reads the account which Mrs. Besant has given of the horror of that terrible time can doubt the reality and sincerity of her struggle against unbelief.

No one who has not felt it knows the fearful agony caused by doubt to the earnestly religious mind. There is in this life no other pain so horrible. The doubt seems to ship-wreck everything, to destroy the one steady gleam of happiness "on the other side" which no earthly storm could obscure; to make all life gloomy with the horror of despair, a darkness that may verily be felt. Fools talk of Atheism as the outcome of foul life and vicious thought. They, in their shallow heartlessness, their brainless stupidity, cannot even dimly imagine the anguish of the mere penumbra of the eclipse, much less of the great darkness in which the orphaned soul cries out into the infinite emptiness: "Is it a devil who has made this world? Are we the sentient toys of an Almighty Power, who sports with our agony, and whose peals of awful mocking laughter echo the wailings of our despair?"

The Horror of Great Darkness

Speaking many years later of the trials of that transition stage, she showed that time had in no sense lessened the bitter memory of that hour of gloom. In a tractate published many years later, she says :

> Last of all I ought to be the one to say that in the renouncel of belief in Christ the God-man, or in the Father of heaven, there is nothing but pain to the earnest heart. Those to whom religion has seemed a reality cannot fail to suffer keenly in the wrench that tears out of the soil wherein it has struck deeply the root of faith. That keen anguish of feeling that we have been building without a solid foundation ; that "horror of great darkness" which falls upon us when we fear lest our God is only a dream of the fancy ; that bitter resentment that springs up on finding that we have been lavishing our heart's treasures of love and devotion upon a phantom ; all this involves agony, which is sharp in proportion to the nobility and tenderness of the sufferer. This is the price we pay for the paradise apples of superstition, which turn to ashes in the mouth. But beyond the struggle and the turmoil, on the other side of the river of doubt, there is a firm ground on which to stand in peace at last.

A Word by the Way

I venture at this point to interrupt Mrs. Besant's narrative in order to insert the following observations suggested, by this autobiography, to one of the most saintly women of contemporary Christendom. From a heart full of sympathy, born of similar suffering, she wrote :

Would that some one with heart and brain and pen could set himself to consider that rock on which Mrs. Besant's faith was first wrecked, but in which she is not alone. All the atheistical women I have known, and I have known a good many, and men too, have run upon that rock and been broken—I mean the error of imagining that there is but one Great Being influencing, managing, and working in the world—only *one*, described by Christians as a Benign Being. If there be only *one* Being, or principle, creative and active, in the world, how *can* we fail to be perplexed, and look in doubt ending in rank rebellion or unbelief ? Not until we recognise that there are two ruling powers in the world can we ever be right in our estimate of, or relation to, the God of love ; never, till we recognise the *dual* government, can we see straight. It is a dual government which is at war now, but with a progressive victory for the benign and blessed One, and defeat (with *our* help) for the malign one. *God suffers*, God wars, God (in Jesus) waits, endures, presses on (asking our poor human, but wonderful, help as fellow-workers with God) to win His battle for Him. It is this view I have had of God ever since I entered into peace. It was He who showed it to me as clear as the day.

I have many a time sat by young mothers tried as Mrs. Besant was by the agony of her baby. My own daughter was killed by a cruel and awful death. If I had thought it *was God did it* I should have hated Him with a deadly hatred. But the Divine word says, "*An enemy hath done this.*" The heart of my God was pained for my heart's pain; He hated the author of my pain, and though I suffered frightfully and was in darkness, I never threw it in God's face that He had killed my child. I wish somebody (of power spiritual) could have said to poor Mrs. Besant what I said to my son and daughter when they wondered how God could let their daughter suffer. "But at any rate," they said, "God could have prevented this evil," to which I boldly answered, "No, my darlings, He could not!" His power is for a season limited by mysterious limitations, which He permits, which He suffers, or bows to (we shall know by and by), for an end which will be more beautiful than any autocratic, all-powerful, undisputed sovereignty could ever be. My children have got over their rebellion. They now know that God—that Jesus—disapproves of every suffering which falls on a little child, that He pities, loves, and feels with us; nay, that He is angry with the malign power who is the author of the suffering. And oh! to have His sympathy thus is surely the sweetest thing in life. It enables us to drink the bitterest cup. Have readers of the Gospel never fathomed the significance of the words of Jesus, "Shall we not heal this woman whom Satan hath bound these eighteen years?" Persons in Mrs. Besant's state would say, "Whom God hath afflicted these eighteen years—this cruel, wretched God of the Christian." And again and again Jesus was grieved and angry with the evil spirit which afflicted men and women. God is not the author of sin, disease, evil, pain, or death. These all come from another source. Some say they are mere accidents, aberrations; no, they are more than that. They are deliberately and maliciously inflicted evil, and our God was from the beginning, and will be to the blessed end, the opponent of the enemy of all His work. God is mending, healing, bringing good out of Satan's bad, making us heroic under pains inflicted by the enemy, walking with us through the flames and the floods of the Evil One's creating, and making us His own royal companions, working and waiting for the final victory. If only some one could have pointed out to Mrs. Besant that it was not God who "tortured her child." Was it God who tortured the demoniac boy whose father brought him to Christ? If it had been God who so cruelly flung that boy on the ground, who made him yell and twist with pain, would God's Son and soul have said the words, "Come out of him, thou foul spirit, and go no more into him"? Some, perhaps, think it a discouraging truth that God's power at present is limited in opposing His adversary and ours.

There is one point at which God's power over evil, pain, and sin becomes irresistible and victorious now on earth, and that is the point at which He meets a human heart and human faith. The meeting and union with God of a human spirit, when that human spirit wills as God wills, is the moment of spiritual conception, so to speak, from which a miracle is born. I mean any spiritual miracle, such as the complete change of heart of a sinner or criminal, or the healing of deadly sickness, or the stilling of a storm at sea, etc., etc. I know this to be true. The Lord said He could not (in a certain town) do many mighty works because of their unbelief, but if He had found faith which would have brought some soul or souls into union with His Divine soul, He could have done many mighty works. It is the most awful, wonderful truth this, *i.e.*, that you can supply to God the conditions which are needful to Him and which He cannot do without, in order to gain a present victory over evil, or work a present spiritual work of miracle. It is the hidden marriage of the divine and the human, by which the new heavens and new earth shall be born.

The Resolve to "Try All Things"

It is not surprising that under the stress of that trial her health gave way, and for weeks she lay prostrate and helpless with terrible head pain that banished sleep, and which the doctors vainly sought to allay by covering her head with ice and dosing her with opium. Not until her mind could be diverted from hell did the pain abate, and one of the means by which her cure was effected was the study of anatomy. An analysis of " Human Osteology " was a curious but for a time a sufficient anodyne. The pain abated, sleep returned, and she was once more able to go about her daily duties. No sooner had she recovered than she set herself to attack, with characteristic intrepidity, the doubts which had assailed her. She says :

I resolved, that whatever might be the result, I would take each dogma of the Christian religion, and carefully and thoroughly examine it, so that I should never say again " I believe " where I had not proved. So, patiently and steadily, I set to work. Four problems chiefly at this time pressed for solution—1. The eternity of punishment after death. 2. The meaning of " goodness " and " love " as applied to a God who had made this world with all its evil and misery. 3. The nature of the atonement of Christ, and the " justice " of God in accepting a vicarious suffering from Christ and a vicarious righteousness from the sinner. 4. The meaning of " inspiration " as applied to the Bible, and the reconciliation of the perfection of the author with the blunders and immoralities of the work.

In the attempt to solve these problems she read Maurice, Robertson of Brighton, and Stopford Brooke. Poetry, beauty, devotion, enthusiasm, she found, but no solid rock on which to build her faith. She tried a course of "Bampton Lectures." Dean Mansel deepened and intensified her doubts, Liddon's "Bampton Lecture" made no impression on her. The more she read the more she doubted. W. R. Greg's *Creeds of Christendom*, Matthew Arnold's *Literature and Dogma*, and Renan's *Vie de Jesus* widened her horizon and made it seem more than ever impossible to crib, cabin, and confine the universe of truth within the ecclesiastic pinfold in which her husband was a duly accredited under shepherd.

Vicar's Wife at Sibsey

Thanks to her representations to her uncle, Lord Hatherley, Mr. Besant had received the Crown living of Sibsey, in Lincoln, valued at £450 per annum, and there the family had been established in the Vicarage. The improvement in their circumstances brought with it an added complication to Mrs. Besant. Imagine a country parson's wife who sympathised with her whole soul with Joseph Arch and rebellious Hodge, while the indignant farmers regarded the Labourers' Union as little short of high treason and red revolution !

Mrs. Besant endeavoured, however, as best she could, to find practical relief in nursing, the work for which she has always had a positive passion. She remarks in her autobiography :

> I think Mother Nature meant me for a nurse, for I take a keen delight in nursing any one, provided only that there is peril in the sickness, so that there is the strange and solemn feeling of the struggle between the human skill we wield and the supreme enemy Death. There is a strange fascination in fighting Death step by step, and then is felt to the full where one fights for life as life, and not for a life one loves.

All Christian Dogmas Go but One

These duties of the parish, however, could not silence the ceaseless strife within. Her health broke down, and she went to London to recover. When there, she found in Mr. Voysey's ministrations "a gleam of light across the stormy sea of doubt and distress," but Theism afforded her only a temporary resting-place. She now definitely rejected what she called all the " barbarous doctrines of the Christian faith," and felt with relief and joy that " they were but the dreams of ignorant and semi-savage minds, not the revelation of a God." One last dogma, however, still remained. Not all her reading of Theodore Parker and Francis Newman and Miss Cobbe had been able to rob her of her faith in the deity of Christ. She clung to it all the more closely because it was the last and to her the dearest of all.

> The doctrine was dear from association ; there was something at once soothing and ennobling in the idea of a union between man and God, between a perfect man and a divine supremacy, between a human heart and an almighty strength. Jesus as God was interwoven with all art, with all beauty in religion ; to break with the deity of Jesus was to break with all music, with painting, with literature, the Divine child in His mother's arms, the Divine man in His passion and in His triumph, the human friend encircled with the majesty of the Godhead. Did inexorable truth demand that this ideal figure, with all its pathos, its beauty, its human love, should pass into the pantheon of the dead gods of the past ?

She at first shrank from beginning an inquiry the result of which might entail upon her, the wife of a clergyman, the necessity of repudiating all pretence of belonging to a Christian Church. Hitherto her warfare had been in secret, her suffering solely mental. But if this last doctrine were to go, " to the inner would be added the outer warfare, and who could say how far this might carry me ? " She shivered for a moment on the brink and then she took the plunge.

The Divinity of Christ

One night only I spent in the struggle over the question, " Shall I examine the claims to deity of Jesus of Nazareth ? " When morning broke the answer was clearly formulated : " Truth is greater than peace or position, If Jesus be God, challenge will not shake His deity ; if He be man, it is blasphemy to worship Him." I re-read Liddon's " Bampton Lectures " on this controversy, and Renan's *Vie de Jesus* ; I studied the Gospels, and tried to represent to myself the life there outlined. I tested the conduct there given as I should have tested the conduct of any ordinary historical character . . . and I saw that, if there were any truth in the Gospels at all, they told a story of a struggling, suffering, sinning, praying man, and not of a God at all, and the dogma of the deity of Christ followed the rest of the Christian doctrines into the limbo of past beliefs.

HER LAST FORLORN HOPE

But before she finally parted with all her Christian faith, she took a step which in itself is sufficient to render her autobiography invaluable to the historian and theologian. There are few pages in contemporary annals more touching, more simple, and more dramatic than those in which Mrs. Besant tells of her pilgrimage to Dr. Pusey to see whether, as a last forlorn hope, the eminent leader of the High Church party might haply be able to save her from the abyss. As probably not one per cent of my readers have ever heard of this historic interview between the old chief priest of Anglican orthodoxy and the young woman who was destined to be the lieutenant of the leader of the party of Revolt against all accepted orthodoxies, I quote it in its entirety.

Yet one other effort I made to save myself from the difficulties I foresaw in connection with this final breach with Christianity. There was one man who had in former days wielded over me a great influence, one whose writings had guided and taught me for many years—Dr. Pusey, the venerable leader of the Catholic party in the Church, the learned patristic scholar, full of the wisdom of antiquity. He believed in Christ as God ; what if I put my difficulties to him ? If he resolved them for me, I should escape the struggle I foresaw ; if he could not resolve them, then no answer to them was to be hoped for. My decision was quickly made : being with my mother, I could write to him unnoticed, and I sat down putting my questions clearly and fully, stating my difficulties, and asking him whether, out of his wider knowledge and deeper reading, he could resolve them for me . . . Dr. Pusey advised me to read Liddon's " Bampton Lectures," referred me to various passages, chiefly from the Fourth Gospel, if I remember rightly, and invited me to go down to Oxford and talk over my difficulties. Liddon's " Bampton Lectures " I had thoroughly studied, and the Fourth Gospel had no weight with me, the arguments in favour of its Alexandrian origin being familiar to me, but I determined to accept his invitation to a personal interview, regarding it as the last chance of remaining in the Church.

A Pilgrimage to Dr. Pusey

To Oxford accordingly I took the train and made my way to the famous doctor's rooms. I was shown in, and saw a short stout gentleman dressed in a cassock, and looking like a comfortable monk ; but the keen eyes, steadfastly gazing into mine, told me of the power and subtlety hidden by the unprepossessing form. The

DR. E. D. PUSEY

head was fine and impressive, the voice low, penetrating, drilled into a somewhat monotonous and artificial subdued tone. I quickly saw that no sort of enlightenment could result from our interview. He treated me as a penitent going to confession, seeking the advice of a director, not as an inquirer struggling after truth, and resolute to find some firm standing ground in the sea of doubt, whether on the shores of orthodoxy or of heresy. He would not deal with the question of the Deity of Christ as a question for argument; he reminded me: "You are speaking of your judge," when I pressed some question. The mere suggestion of an imperfection in Jesus' character made him shudder in positive pain, and he checked me with raised hand and the rebuke: "You are blaspheming; the very thought is a terrible sin."

"You Have Read Too Much Already!"

I asked him if he could recommend me any books that would throw light upon the subject: "No, no, you have read too much already. You must pray, you must pray." Then, as I said I could not believe without proof, I was told: "Blessed are they that have not seen, and yet have believed"; and my further questioning was checked by the murmur: "O my child, how undisciplined! how impatient!" Truly, he must have found in me—hot, eager, passionate in my determination to know, resolute not to profess belief when belief was absent—but very little of that meek, chastened, submissive spirit, which he was accustomed in the penitents wont to seek his counsel as a spiritual guide. In vain did he bid me pray as though I believed; in vain did he urge the duty of blind submission to the authority of the Church, of yielding, unreasoning faith, which received but questioned not. He had no conception of the feelings of the sceptical spirit; his own faith was solid as a rock—firm, satisfied, unshakeable. He would as soon have committed suicide as doubted the infallibility of the "universal Church."

"At Your Peril You Reject It!"

"It is not your duty to ascertain the truth," he told me sternly. "It is your duty to accept and believe the truth as laid down by the Church; at your peril you reject it; the responsibility is not yours so long as you dutifully accept what the Church has laid down for your acceptance. Did not the Lord promise that the presence of the Spirit should be ever with His Church, to guide her into all truth?"

"But the fact of the promise and its value are the very points on which I am doubtful," I answered.

He shuddered. "Pray, pray," he said; "Father, forgive her, for she knows not what she says."

It was in vain I urged I had everything to gain and nothing to lose by following his directions, but that it seemed to me that fidelity to truth forbade a pretended acceptance of that which was not believed.

"Everything to lose? Yes, indeed. You will be lost for time and lost for eternity."

"Lost or not," I rejoined, "I must and will find out what is true, and I will not believe until I am sure."

"You have no right to make terms with God," he answered, "as to what you will believe and what you will not believe. You are full of intellectual pride."

"I Forbid You to Speak of Your Disbelief"

I sighed hopelessly. Little feeling of pride was there in me just then, and I felt that in this rigid unyielding dogmatism there was no comprehension of my difficulties, no help for my strugglings. I rose, and, thanking him for his courtesy, said that I would not waste his time further, that I must go home and just face the difficulties out, openly leaving the Church and taking the consequences. Then for the first time his serenity was ruffled.

"I forbid you to speak of your disbelief," he cried; "I forbid you to lead into your own lost state the souls for whom Christ died."

Slowly and sadly I took my way back to the railway station, knowing that my last chance of escape had failed me.

The die was cast. "The ideal figure, with all its pathos, its beauty, its human love," passed from her "into the pantheon of the dead gods of the past."

Christian No Longer

Mrs. Besant was "still heartily Theistic," but she could no longer take Holy Communion. With a feeling of deadly sickness she rose and went out of church when the sacrament was administered to the communicants. Good farmers' wives felt sure she was ill, and called next day with sympathising inquiries. Alas, her sickness was beyond their treatment! She set to work on her first controversial tract, which Mr. Thomas Scott of Upper Norwood published anonymously as "by the wife of a beneficed clergyman," but which was subsequently republished as the first chapter in *My Path to Atheism*. Other pamphlets followed. In 1873 her health broke down again. A relative of her husband, who mercifully remains unknown in anonymity, urged that although it was true that all educated people (!) held the same views which she expressed, pressure should be put upon her to induce her to conform to the outward ceremonies of the Church and to attend the

Holy Communion. This, says Mrs. Besant, "I was resolved not to do, whatever might be the result of my 'obstinacy.'"

Expelled from Home

It was resolved, on the other hand, that she should either resume attendance at the Communion or should not return home. Hypocrisy or expulsion—such was the alternative. She chose the latter. Her mother, whom she loved as she loved nothing else on earth, begged her on her knees to yield. But to live a lie? Not even for mother was that possible. Mrs. Besant was herself a mother. The two little ones who worshipped her, and to whom she was mother, nurse, and playfellow, these also might have to be sacrificed; both ultimately were sacrificed, but for a while one was spared to her.

Of the causes which enabled Mrs. Besant to secure for a time the custody of her daughter, she has spoken guardedly in her autobiography, and she refuses now to speak at all. "It was eighteen years ago," she replied to my inquiries; "should there not be a statute of limitations for such things?" But we gather, not obscurely, from her autobiography that it was she who had legal ground for action against Mr. Besant. She says :

> Facts (which I have not touched on in this record) came accidentally to my brother's knowledge, and he resolved that I should have the protection of legal separation, and not be turned wholly penniless and alone into the world. When everything was arranged, I found myself possessed of complete personal freedom and of a small monthly income sufficient for respectable starvation.

THE DEED OF SEPARATION

She was then a young woman of twenty-six. Five years afterwards she was deprived of the custody of the child, because she propagated the principles of Atheism, and published the *Fruits of Philosophy*. Sir George Jessel, who was brutally rude when hearing the case, and guilty of gross inaccuracy, to say the least of it, in his judgment, advised her to file a claim for divorce or judicial separation. Mrs. Besant says :

> The claim filed alleged distinct acts of cruelty, and I brought witnesses to support the claim, among them the doctor who had attended me during my married life. Mr. Ince filed an answer of general denial, adding that the acts of cruelty, if any, were done in the "heat

of the moment." He did not, however, venture to contest the case, although I tendered myself for cross-examination, but pleaded the deed of separation as a bar to further proceedings. This view Sir G. Jessel upheld. The nett result of the proceedings was that, had I gone to the Divorce Courts in 1873, I might at least have obtained a divorce *a mensa et thoro.*

Unfortunately, the deed of separation, which was no bar to her husband wresting from her the possession of the child which the deed promised her, was an absolute bar to a judicial separation. The deed shielded him, but left her at his mercy. That is all that I can say on this painful subject, to which it was necessary to advert, if only in order to call attention to the fact that never, in all the prolonged litigations in which Mrs. Besant has been engaged, has there ever been any imputation cast upon her personal character. For whatever breach of conjugal contract there was she has not to answer. And since the separation, although she has been tracked by detectives, enveloped in a cloud of scandal, and made the mark for every reckless calumniator, no human being has ever ventured to stand up in public and attempt to substantiate a single accusation against the character of Mrs. Besant.

III. ATHEIST

Mrs. Besant was now fairly launched. She was a lady unattached, with a baby daughter to look after, and a small annuity. She went to live with her mother, who was also in straitened circumstances, and passed through the usual dismal experience of the gentlewoman seeking employment. She found little work of the paying kind, except occasional nursing, and the writing of free-thought pamphlets for Mr. Scott. After a year, her mother sickened and came near to death. This brought Mrs. Besant into personal contact with another of the famous Churchmen of the Victorian era, and her description of her visit to Dean Stanley is a fitting pendant and contrast to that which she gave of her visit to Dr. Pusey. This is how it came about.

At this period, after eighteen months of abstention, and for the last time, I took the Sacrament. This statement will seem strange to my readers, but the matter happened in this wise.

Her Last Communion

My dear mother had an intense longing to take it, but absolutely refused to do so unless I partook of it with her. "If it be necessary to salvation," she persisted doggedly, "I will not take it if my darling Annie is to be shut out; I would rather be lost with her than saved without her." In vain I urged that I could not take it without telling the officiating clergyman of my heresy, and that under such circumstances the clergyman would be sure to refuse to administer to me. She insisted that she could not die happy if I did not take it with her. I went to a clergyman whom I knew well and laid the case before him; as I expected, he refused to allow me to communicate. I tried a second; the result was the same. I was in despair, to me the service was foolish and superstitious, but I would have done a great deal more for my mother than eat bread and drink wine, provided the eating and drinking did not, on pretence of faith on my part, soil my honesty. At last a thought struck me, there was Dean Stanley, my mother's favourite, a man known to be of the broadest school within the Church of England; suppose I asked him. . .

A Pilgrimage to Dean Stanley

I told no one, but set out resolutely for the Deanery Westminster, timidly asked for the Dean, and followed the servant upstairs with a sinking heart. I was left for a moment alone in the library, and then the Dean came in. I don't think I ever in my life felt more intensely uncomfortable than I did in that minute's interval, as he stood waiting for me to speak, his clear, grave, piercing eyes gazing right into mine.

Very falteringly I preferred my request, very boldly stating that I was not a believer in Christ, that my mother was dying, and that she was fretting to take the sacrament; that she would not take it unless I took it with her; that two clergymen had not allowed me to take part in the service; that I had come to him in despair, feeling how great was the intrusion, but—she was dying.

"You are quite right to come to me," he said, as I concluded, in that soft, musical voice of his, his keen gaze having changed into one no less direct but marvellously gentle. "Of course I will go and see your mother, and I have little doubt that if you will not mind talking over your position with me, we may see clear to doing as your mother wishes."

I could barely speak my thanks, so much did the kindly sympathy move me; the revulsion from anxiety and fear of rebuff was strong enough to be almost pain. But Dean Stanley did more than I asked. He suggested that he should call that afternoon and have a quiet chat with my mother, and then come the following day to administer the Sacrament.

"A stranger's presence is always trying to a sick person," he said, with a rare delicacy of thought;

"and joined to the excitement of the service it might be too much for your dear mother. If I spend half an hour with her to-day, and administer the Sacrament to-morrow, it will, I think, be better for her."

Dean Stanley's Test of a Christian

So Dean Stanley came that afternoon, and remained talking with my mother for about half an hour, and then set himself to understand my position. He finally told me that conduct was far more important than theory, and that he regarded all as "Christian" who recognised and tried to follow the moral law. On the question of the absolute deity of Jesus he laid but little stress. Jesus was "in a special sense" the "Son of God," but it was folly to jangle about words with only human meanings when dealing with the mysteries of divine existence, and above all it was folly to make such words into dividing lines between earnest souls. The one important matter was the recognition of "duty to God and man," and all who were one in that recognition might rightfully join in an act of worship, the essence of which was not acceptance of dogma, but love of God and self-sacrifice for man. "The Holy Communion," he said, in his soft tones, "was never meant to divide from each other hearts that are searching after the one true God; it was meant by its Founder as a symbol of unity, not of strife."

"Remember the Honest Search for Truth Can Never Displease the God of Truth"

On the following day he came again and celebrated the "Holy Communion" by the bedside of my dear mother. Well, I was repaid for the great struggle it had cost me to ask so great a kindness from a stranger when I saw the comfort the gentle noble heart had given to my mother. He soothed away all her anxiety about my heresy with tactful wisdom, bidding her have no fear of difference of opinion where the heart was set on truth. "Remember," she told me he had said to her, "remember our God is the God of truth, and that therefore the honest search for truth can never be displeasing in His eyes."

Dean Stanley and the Church

Once again after that he came, and after his visit to my mother we had a long talk. I ventured to ask him, the conversation having turned that way, how, with views so broad as his own, he found it possible to remain in communion with the Church of England. "I think," he said, gently, "I am of more service to religion by remaining in the Church and striving to widen its boundaries from within than if I left it and worked from without." And he went on to explain how as Dean of Westminster he was in a rarely independent

DEAN STANLEY

position, and could make the Abbey of a wider national service than would otherwise be possible. In all he said on this his love and his pride in the glorious Abbey were manifest, and it was easy to see that old historical association, love of music, of painting, of stately architecture, were the bonds that held him to the "old historic Church of England." His emotions, not his intellect, kept him Churchman, and he shrunk with the over-sensitiveness of the cultured scholar from the idea of allowing the old traditions to be handled roughly by inartistic hands. Naturally of a refined and delicate nature—and he had been rendered yet more sensitive by the training of the college and the court—the exquisite courtesy of his manner was but the high polish of a naturally gentle and artistic spirit, a spirit whose gentleness sometimes veiled its strength.

Naturally Mrs. Besant was grateful. But when I told Canon Liddon the circumstance in one of our Monday afternoon walks on the Embankment, he almost shuddered with horror at the sacrilege to which he conceived the Dean had been a guilty party.

The much-loved mother soon passed away, declaring almost with her dying breath that "Annie's troubles would all come from her being too religious." Grotesquely absurd as the observation appeared to those who saw in Mrs. Besant only the high priestess of infidelity, it was the religiousness of her irreligion that alone made the latter formidable.

Mrs. Besant's First Speech

It was shortly after her mother's death that Mrs. Besant first began to speak in public. Her first speech—the speech which revealed to her that she had the gift of speech—was delivered when she was still at Sibsey in the parish church. It occurred in this way:

> In the spring of 1873 I delivered my first lecture. It was delivered to no one, queer as that may sound to my readers. And indeed it was queer altogether. I was learning to play the organ, and was in the habit of practising in the church by myself, without a blower. One day, being securely locked in, I thought I should like to try how it "felt" to speak from the pulpit . . . So, queer as it may seem, I ascended the pulpit in a big, empty, lonely church, and there and then I delivered my first lecture. I shall never forget the feeling of power and of delight that came upon me as my voice rolled down the aisles, and the passion in me broke into balanced sentences, and never paused for rhythmical expression, while I felt that all I wanted was to see the church full of upturned faces, instead of the emptiness of the silent pews. And as though in a dream the solitude became peopled, and I saw the eager eyes and

the listening faces ; and as the sentences came unbidden from my lips, and my own tones echoed back to me from the pillars of the ancient church, I knew of a verity that the gift of speech was mine, and that if ever—and it seemed to me impossible then—if ever the chance came to me of public work, that at least this power of melodious utterance should win hearing for the message I had to bring. . . . And indeed none can know, save those who have felt it, what joy there is in the full rush of language which moves and sways ; to feel the crowd respond to the lightest touches ; to see the faces brighten or graven at your bidding ; to know that the sources of human passion and human emotion gush at the word of the speaker, as the stream from the riven rock ; to feel that the thought that thrills through a thousand hearers had its impulse from you and throbs back to you the fuller from a thousand heartbeats : is there any joy in life more brilliant than this, fuller of passionate triumph, and of the very essence of intellectual delight ?

It was not until the following year that she made her appearance as a public lecturer, her first subject being "The Political Status of Women," but this is slightly anticipating.

Hard Times

After her mother died her struggles for existence became harder. Often she would go out to study at the British Museum, "so as to have my dinner in town," the said dinner being conspicuous by its absence. She says:

> I can now look on them without regret. More, I am glad to have passed through them, for they taught me how to sympathise with those who are struggling as I struggled then, and I can never hear the words fall from pale lips, "I am hungry," without remembering how painful a thing hunger is, and without curing the pain, at least for a moment.

A fellow-feeling makes one wondrous kind. If she had not hungered then, she would probably not be Socialist now.

From Theism into Atheism

She was still Theist, but the Theism was wearing very thin. She attended Moncure Conway's lectures at South Place Chapel, and after reading Mansel's "Bampton Lecture" and Mill's *Examination of Sir W. Hamilton's Philosophy*, she plunged into a pretty severe study of Comte's *Philosophie Positive*. She gave up the use of prayer, and as she finely says:

> God fades gradually out of the daily life of those who never pray; a God who is not a providence is a

superfluity; when from the heavens does not smile a listening Father, it soon becomes an empty space, whence resounds no echo of man's cry.

Thus she gravitated naturally and of necessity into Atheism. It was, however, left to Mr. Bradlaugh, to whom her attention was first called by Mr. Conway, to reveal to her that she had really and logically become an Atheist without knowing it. She bought a *National Reformer* one day at Mr. Truelove's shop, and from it learnt that the National Secular Society was an organisation for the propagandism of Freethought. She wrote to Mr. Bradlaugh, was accepted as a member, and on August 2nd, 1874, went to hear him for the first time at the Hall of Science.

Her First Sight of Mr. Bradlaugh

The grave quiet strong look, the broad forehead and the massive head, of Mr. Bradlaugh impressed her much, and a day or two later she went at his invitation to discuss with him the all-engrossing subject. "You have thought yourself into Atheism without knowing it," said he. A few days later he offered her a small weekly salary and a place on the staff of the *National Reformer*. She adopted the nom-de-plume "Ajax," and then began a journalistic career the end of which is not yet. There also was begun an almost ideal affectionate friendship between Mr. Bradlaugh and herself, which terminated only with the grave—if indeed it can be said to have terminated then. Of that, however, we need not speak. Mrs. Besant's noble tribute to her deceased friend must still be fresh in the memory of all my readers.

Another Observation by the Way

Here again I venture to interrupt the narrative to insert the comments of a woman whose spiritual experience in some things resembles Mrs. Besant's, although, as her letter shows, it differed widely both in its methods and its results.

One thing in Mrs. Besant makes me wonder. She is a far stronger, more intellectual person than I, a giantess in a certain sense, and yet I see in her what seems a weakness, one which I, though an inferior person, was never tempted to fall into. I mean that way of going to man for light and guidance instead of God. In the deepest darkness and agony of spirit, in the moment when she felt the world was slipping from beneath her feet (I know well the suffering she describes), she went after Pusey, Arthur Stanley, Bradlaugh. It was always a good man, but a man, and she got nothing from them. Naturally to a mind like hers it was only feeding on husks to hear the advice of even the best of men. I never went for help to a man in my life. I had years of spiritual conflict. I knew intimately Pusey, Stanley, and a number of other lights, good and wise men, but I had always the strongest instinctive conviction that no human teacher could possibly fathom my case ; besides, my very soul cried out for nothing less than the living God. If I could not get face to face with Him, I must perish in darkness. I should have thought it a miserable weakness even to consult the best of men. My years of "hell on earth" were hidden in my own breast. I went to seek God night after night through the whole night. I must have it out with Him and Him alone. If He was not I should get no answer. If He existed, I thought I might get an answer, and at last I did. It was an awful experience, but how everlastingly blessed the result ! Nothing could shake me after I had met Him and heard Him speak, but if I had spoiled the whole business by going to any man, or woman, or saint, on earth, I should have been a poor creature. The question comes to me, "How could so powerful and independent a being as Mrs. Besant stoop to go for spiritual aid to any man, if she at all believed there was a God ?" May she now be guided at last into the presence of the great and awful "Father of Spirits" and Father of Humanity, and never again draw water from any lower fountain.

The Sacred Cause of Freethought

In January, 1875, Mrs. Besant, after delivering a lecture at South Place Chapel, "The True Basis of Morality," which has since obtained a circulation of 70,000, became one of the regular lecturers of the Secular Society. Writing in 1885, she said :

Never have I felt one hour's regret for the resolution taken in solitude in January, 1875, to devote to that sacred cause every power of brain and tongue that I possessed. Not lightly was that resolution taken, for I know no task of weightier responsibility than that of standing forth as teacher, and swaying thousands of hearers year after year. But I pledged my word to the cause I loved that no effort on my part should be wanting to render myself worthy of the privilege of service which I took ; that I would read, and study, and train every faculty that I had ; that I would polish my language, discipline my thought, widen my knowledge ; and this at least I may say, that if I have written and spoken much, I have studied and thought more, and that, at least, I have not given to my mistress Liberty that "which hath cost me nothing."

ANNIE BESANT: 1876

The doctor told her that her chest was delicate, and that lecturing would either kill or cure her. The result proves that—as John Wesley and General Booth have always maintained—there is no medicine like speaking in the open air for a delicate chest. She continued to write for the *National Reformer*, and from time to time did extra literary work. She compiled, for instance, a secular song book, and undertook a close study of "two cabsful of books on the French Revolution," in order to deliver a course of lectures on that time. "The Revolution became to me as a drama in which I had myself taken part, and the actors therein became personal friends and foes."

The "Fruits of Philosophy"

So passed two years away, and then, in 1877, she stumbled, as it were, almost unwittingly, into one of the most important and far-reaching of all the controversies with which her name has been associated. The stand which, together with Mr. Bradlaugh, she took in vindicating the right to print and publish physiological works, discussing the best method of checking the over multiplication of the population of the planet, led her, almost without intending it, into the heart of the neo-Malthusian controversy. This action of hers, from whatever point we regard it, was one of the bravest of her life. Whatever view may be taken of the question whether or not it is wise or right to allow conscience and reason to have any control over the most momentous of all the acts which human beings can perform, there can be no doubt that it is virtually criminal to allow any persons to marry until they clearly understand what marriage means, what it entails, and what moral questions its responsibilities raise. In an ideal state, the clergyman or registrar who ventured to solemnise a marriage within less than one month of the issue, by their parents or guardians, to the intending bride and bridegroom, of a judicious and scientific treatise on the physiology of the state into which they propose to enter should be sent to gaol without the option of a fine. Yet because Mr. Bradlaugh and Mrs. Besant insisted upon vindicating the right to print a work discussing the question, they have been pilloried as malefactors whose offence is so heinous as to exclude them for ever from decent society. That is all cant, and very cruel cant. Whatever mistakes in science or in morals there may have been in Knowlton's book, the whole sum of them did not amount to the monstrous wickedness of allowing young persons to bind themselves for life in a contract the very first conditions of which they have never had any opportunity of understanding.

The Morality of Her Position

It is particularly abominable that they should have been assailed on the score of morality. The alternative to neo-Malthusianism is Malthus pure and simple. The neo-Malthusian declares that early marriages and small families are the formulæ alike of civilisation and of morality. The Malthusian declares that marriage must be postponed in order that the increase of the population may be reduced, which, as a practical matter of fact, means that with most men prostitution will be substituted for marriage. The moment we pass from the preliminary question on which Mrs. Besant and Mr. Bradlaugh first took their stand as to the freedom of printing, the only question at issue between them and their opponents is as to the comparative disadvantages of late marriage plus prostitution and early marriage plus preventive checks on the limitless multiplication of children.

The Summing Up of the Lord Chief Justice

That this was the case was clearly stated by the Lord Chief Justice in the admirably lucid summing-up, which would have secured an acquittal from any jury if there had not been a strong prejudice against the Atheist.

> Dr. Knowlton suggests—and here we come to the critical point of this inquiry—he suggests that instead of marriage being postponed it shall be hastened. He suggests that marriage should take place in the heyday of life, when the passions are at their highest, and that the evils of over-population shall be remedied by persons after they have married, having recourse to artificial means to prevent the procreation of a numerous offspring, and the consequent evils, especially to the poorer classes, which the production of a too numerous offspring is certain to bring about.

The Jury condemned the book as calculated to deprave public morals, although the Lord Chief Justice told them that every medical work was open to the same imputation, and entirely exonerated the defendants of any corrupt motives in publishing it.

The Sentence and Its Sequel

If the defendants had bowed to this decision, they would have been allowed to go scot-free. As they declared their determination to set it at defiance—for it is only by martyrdom that certain kinds of oppression can be prevented—they were sentenced to six months as first-class misdemeanants, fined £200 each, and ordered to give recognisances for £500 each that they would not publish the book for two years. Mr. Bradlaugh, however, appealed to the Court of Appeal on a point of law, which being decided in their favour, the whole proceedings were quashed. The victory was decisive. Knowlton's pamphlet was again largely circulated, till a statement was conveyed to the defendants that no further prosecution would be attempted. It was then withdrawn, only to be replaced by another from the pen of Mrs. Besant, of which 100,000 copies have been sold in Europe and 110,000 in America. It has been translated into six languages, and has gone the round of the civilised world. Against this no prosecution has ever been taken.

Whose Is the Fault?

That evil has followed the wholesale circulation of *The Law of Population: Its Consequences and Its Bearing on Human Conduct*, it is impossible to deny. But that it is an advantage, altogether out-weighing all conceivable disadvantages, that the most momentous of all questions should be intelligently discussed by those whom it most concerns instead of being burked in ignorance, and that an attempt at least should be made to bring the most vital of all departments of human conduct under some guidance superior to that of mere animal instinct, are propositions which can hardly be gainsaid.

Mrs. Besant's Views on Marriage

The popular calumny that the *Fruits of Philosophy* advocated free love is a malignant falsehood. Mrs. Besant, so far from having advocated free love, has always preached and practised a much higher standard of morality in these matters than most of her censors. As she put it long ago in her writings :

> No countenance is given to those who fain would destroy the idea of the durable union between one man and one woman. Monogamy appears to me to be the result of civilisation, of personal dignity, of cultured feeling ; loyalty of one man to one woman is, to me, the highest sexual ideal. The more civilised the nature the more durable and exclusive does the marriage union become . . . Hence it arises that true marriage is exclusive, and that prostitution is revolting to the noble of both sexes, since in prostitution love is shorn of its fairest attributes, and passion, which is only his wings, is made the sole representative of the divinity. The fleeting connections supposed by free-love theorists are steps backward and not forward ; they offer no possibility of home, no education of character, no guarantee for the training of the children. The culture both of the father and the mother, of the two natures of which its own is the resultant, is necessary to the healthy development of the child. It cannot be deprived of either without injury to its full and perfect growth.

There is not a semblance of truth in the assertion that Dr. Knowlton, in the *Fruits of Philosophy*, advocated promiscuity. The Lord Chief Justice branded this as a lie, although Sir George Jessel did not hesitate to pick up the falsehood in order to excuse the outrage which he legally accomplished when he wrested the daughter from her mother's arms. Lord Coleridge told the present Lord Chancellor, who was then Solicitor-General, that his statement that the book was intended to justify free love at the expense of marriage, was an unjust accusation for which he could only find the excuse that the man who made it had not half-studied the book. He went on :

> I must say that I believe that every word he says about marriage being a desirable institution, and every word he says with reference to the enjoyments and happiness it engenders, is said as honestly and truly as anything probably ever uttered by man.

Such a dictum might have sufficed, but, unfortunately, it did not suffice to close the mouths of clerical and other libellers, some of whom had to smart for their calumnies in the courts of law.

A Legal Outrage

Of those who went down to the grave unwhipped of justice, Sir George Jessel is conspicuous. His brutality was equalled by his insolence. Like some others who might be named, he seemed to believe that there is no necessity for a judge to be a gentleman, nor did he even take the pains to speak the truth. He may have been right in interpreting the law when he decreed that an Atheist mother ought to be deprived of the care of her daughter at the suit of the very father who, by a legal deed of separation, consigned his daughter to the mother's care, but there was no excuse for the unfeeling and inhuman fashion in which he handled the matter. Mrs. Besant offered to pay £110 a year for the maintenance and education of the child, if it were taken from her, if it could be consigned to some third person not its father. Sir George Jessel, in pronouncing judgment, expressly declared that "Mrs. Besant had been kind and affectionate in her conduct and behaviour towards the child, and had taken the greatest possible care of her so far as regards her physical welfare." The child was ill. Her health was weak. Medical evidence was offered that it was absolutely necessary that she should have her mother's care. Everything was disregarded.

Mother and Daughter

After this it is not surprising that Mrs. Besant's health gave way. She was ordered to have access to her daughter once a month. But the visit upset the child so much, and it was made so odious by its guardians—a clergyman and his wife—that, in mercy to her daughter, she waived her rights.

> I resolved neither to see nor to write to my children until they were old enough to understand and to judge for themselves, and I know I shall win my daughter back in her womanhood, though I have been robbed of her childhood. By effacing myself then I saved her from a constant and painful struggle unfitted for childhood's passionate feelings, and left her only a memory that she loves, undefaced by painful remembrances of her mother insulted in her presence.

This confidence was justified. Miss Mabel Besant is with her mother to-day, and has been with her, contrary to the direction of Sir George Jessel, for the last year and a half. Her education suffered by her enforced sojourn with those who tore her from her mother. Twice Mrs. Besant offered to bear the whole expense of her education in the High School, Cheltenham, or in some London College, without in any way, appearing in the matter, but each time her offer was rudely and insultingly refused. Is it so very surprising that during the years that followed Mrs. Besant felt and spoke and wrote bitterly of the pseudo-Christianity in whose name such things were done ?

IV. SOCIALISM

UPON the phase in her career that filled up the years between 1878 and 1886 I need not dwell. Mrs. Besant wrote and spoke constantly in defence of Atheism, and in support of Radical politics. She was the ablest and most eloquent of all Mr. Bradlaugh's lieutenants ; nor was she only a lieutenant. She was his most trusted, most unselfish friend, whose confidence and affection supplied the chief part of the poetry and the charm of his somewhat austere and militant life.

In religion she was wandering in the wilderness, conscious that for her there could be no return to the fleshpots of Egypt, and not venturing to hope that for her there was any Promised Land.

Therefore, as is the fashion with such souls, she passionately endeavoured to persuade herself that the Sinaitic desert was itself the promised Canaan, or wilderness which would bloom with

ANNIE BESANT : 1884

roses as a garden if only it were judiciously cultivated by Secularist and Radical gardeners, who would extirpate the scrub and the wormwood of obsolete superstition.

"A Nobler Temple and a Grander Creed"

Here is a passage from one of her speeches in antagonism to Christianity, which illustrates the rhythmic music of her utterance, and the kind of consolation with which, in the midst of her destroying career, she sought to satisfy her soul. After a brilliant sketch of the civilisation of the Old World, she continues :

> Such were the might, and the glory, and the beauty of pagan Greece and Rome. And now Christianity is born—born in Judæa, among an ignorant and barbarous people. Christ comes with words of love on his lips and a destroying sword in his hand. See the cross is in the hand of his servant the Church, and she goes among the poor, and her influence spreads until she climbs the throne of the Caesars. And now she bears the crucifix in one hand and the sword in the other, and she reigns from the Imperial throne. The crucifix is her symbol, and look at it well. A dead man hangs on the cross, turning men's thoughts to death instead of life. See from his riven side flow water and blood—

water for the tears that shall be shed for his sake, blood for the lives that shall be spilled for his name. See how she walks over Europe, the cross in her hand! The land is as the Garden of Eden before her, but behind her a desolate wilderness. The arts decay; the schools disappear; all knowledge is withered at the breath of the Church. Intellectual death everywhere meets our eyes. Gloom and darkness envelope Christianity—darkness only lighted up by the lurid flames of the stake where the heretic is burning, and yet more lurid flame of the hell beyond the grave. But see, there is a gleam of light breaking through the sky. It comes from Spain, where the followers of the false prophet are. Science is born, new born to bless the earth. But round the cradle of the infant Hercules gather the serpents of the Church; they hiss, and bite, and struggle. Their fangs are the dungeon and the stake, and the child is in sore peril of life; but he fights and catches the hydra necks and strangles them, and the serpents cannot longer bite. Yet the struggle is not over: it continues even till to-day. The crucifix is stricken to the earth, the sword is broken and dashed from the hands of the Church. It can no longer touch the body: it can only cramp the soul. But we will free the souls of men as we have freed their bodies. Instead of religion we will give them science. Instead of heaven we will give them earth. Instead of credulity we will give them knowledge. Instead of fear we will give them love. Love on earth which Christianity has darkened, instead of fear of hell, which churches have dreamed. We raise a nobler temple and we bring a grander creed. Our morality is based on experience, not on revelation ; on man's needs, not on God's commands. Thus at length shall the world regain its old beauty, and it shall be beautiful because it shall be consecrated to man, and shall no longer be darkened because it belongs to God.

Her Moral Teaching

It will be noted that Mrs. Besant here, as always, spoke, not as the advocate of licence, but as the priestess of a higher and more exacting morality than that of the conventional religion. If she attacked Christianity, she borrowed her most effective weapon from the Christian armoury. It was with the lofty ideal of the Nazarene that she pierced the hide of the blatant beast of intolerant and inconsistent orthodoxy. Here is another passage from one of the most widely circulated of her lectures, written in 1875, which brings out into still clearer relief this passionate aspiration after a really Christ-like morality :

Amid the fervid movement of society, with its wild theories and crude social reforms, with its religious fury against oppression and its unconsidered notions of wider freedom and gladder life, it is of vital importance that morality should stand on a foundation unshakeable; and so through all political and religious revolutions human life may grow purer and nobler, may rise upwards into settled freedom, and not sink downwards into anarchy. Only utility can afford us a sure basis, the reasonableness of which will be accepted alike by the thoughtful student and hard-headed artisan. Utility appeals to all alike, and sets in action motives which are found equally in every human heart. Well shall it be for humanity that creeds and dogmas pass away, that superstition vanishes, that the clear light of freedom and science dawns on a regenerated earth, but well only if men draw tighter the links of trustworthiness, of honour, and of truth. Equality before the law is necessary and just; liberty is the birthright of every man and woman; free individual development will elevate the race and glorify it. But little worth these priceless jewels, little worth liberty and equality, with all their promise for mankind, little worth even wider happiness, if that happiness be selfish, if true fraternity, true brotherhood, do not knit man to man and heart to heart, in loyal service of the common need and generous self-sacrifice to the common good.

Some of Her Writings

Some idea of her literary activity and the range of her studies may be gained from a glance at the catalogue of her publications. She translated

Professor Ludwig Buchner's work on *Mind in Animals*, published the *Freethinkers' Text Book*, wrote a *History of the French Revolution*, compiled a *vade mecum* for Liberationists under the title *Disestablish the Church, or the Sins of the Church of England*; edited a Young Folks' Library of Legends and Tales, which range from the myth of Persephone down to the story of Giordano Bruno; issued an illustrated popular treatise on *Light, Heat, and Sound*, and a short résumé of Positivism for the general reader. Besides there were tracts innumerable on all sorts of subjects, from the Afghan War to the C. D. Acts, *Marriage as It Is and as It Ought to Be*, and *Free Trade and Fair Trade*. She was continually contributing to the *National Reformer*, holding public debates on religion and politics, travelling all round the country lecturing, generally leading the life of a suffragan bishop in the great diocese of the nation which had Mr. Bradlaugh as its episcopal head.

Progress to Socialism

All these years I had never met her. I had spoken up for her as best I could in the *Northern*

Echo at the time of the "Fruits of Philosophy" prosecution and after coming to London I had made a fruitless attempt to make her acquaintance, knowing by a sort of instinct that whenever we did meet we should be good friends. It was not till the time of the Trafalgar Square agitation that we met. That was five years ago. A good deal has happened since then, but whatever ups and downs there have been have only deepened the conviction which I formed when I met her, that there are few living women who have in them more of some elements of the Christian saint than this fiery assailant of the Christian creed. She has become a Socialist, and she is now a Theosophist. If she became a Catholic or a Swedenborgian it would in no way deepen my conviction as to her sterling goodness. There is in her a passion for truth and justice and liberty such as is only found in the elect souls of humanity. She has that rare hunger for self-sacrifice which is the Divine benediction of the Christlike souls. I have had the good fortune to know many of the best women of our day, but I do not know three to whom I would turn with more confidence if I wanted a perfectly faithful expression of what on the whole I should expect to be the mind of Christ on any practical question of life and action.

At the time of the Trafalgar Square trouble she was in deep waters. Her Radicalism was gradually changing into Socialism, and the development was bringing with it estrangement from many old friends, and what was most painful of all, was forcing her unwillingly into a position of antagonism to Mr. Bradlaugh. Mr. Bradlaugh was a Socialist without knowing it. His favourite scheme for transferring all the waste land of the country from its present owners to the nation was essentially socialistic, both in its essence and in the method by which it was to be carried out. Mrs. Besant went on from that proposition to the nationalisation of the land, and from the nationalisation of the land to the nationalisation of capital. The process was one of general development, nor did she really discover that she was a Socialist until she heard Mr. Bradlaugh attack Socialism. But when she saw how things were going she had a very bitter moment. Was it to be ever thus? Was she always to be doomed to have to choose between her convictions and her affections? But the great saying ever sounded in her soul, "Whoso loveth father or mother or friends more than Me is not worthy of Me," and she obeyed.

The Crisis Once More

But with what heart wrench and what black misgivings she once more prepared for her exodus, few can realise but those who have had to answer in simple earnest the searching question, "Lovest thou Me more than these?" Socialism for Mrs. Besant meant once more fronting the world with poverty, it might be with very dire poverty, as a life companion. It meant the severing of old ties, the parting with those who had knit themselves into her life, and it meant going out to face the unknown future with a set of untried comrades, some of whom, to put it mildly, were not exactly the kind of men with whom you would venture into the high places of the fight. When a Christian is in such a position he has the consolations and promises of Christianity to encourage him to choose the right and narrow path. But for her there shone no guiding star amid the gloom. Her health was much impaired, and in the autumn of 1886 I think she would have rejoiced with joy exceeding if she could have been trampled out of life in defending the right of the people to the democratic forum of London in Trafalgar Square.

TRAFALGAR SQUARE

Even the Red Cross Knight in her favourite *Faerie Queen* once fell into the loathly grasp of the hideous monster Despair ; and small wonder if she, who had no red cross on her shield, was for a season captive in the giant's cave. Trafalgar Square roused her out of the gloom. The work of caring for the victims of that police outrage gave her a fresh stimulus to service in the cause of the poor and the oppressed, and it supplied her with new comrades, and thus once more light gleamed through the darkness. It was during these days of trial and suffering and service I saw most of Mrs. Besant. We were both members of the Law and Liberty League, which was formed to provide political prisoners with legal help, to assist the families of the prisoners for liberty, and to form a rallying point for sufferers from oppression. We started together a little halfpenny weekly called the *Link*, a journal for the servants of Man, the central feature of which was that no leading article had to appear which we could not jointly sign. Side by side with other stalwarts we marched across London with Linnell's corpse, in a funeral procession the like of which London had seldom seen, and at the open grave of another martyr to police brutality—a secularist buried without religious rite or words of consolation—I publicly gave Mrs. Besant the right hand of fellowship in the name of Him who came to seek and to save the least of these His brethren. And if I mention this it is only in order to strengthen the weight of my personal testimony, when I say that in all these trying months, when we were constantly together, I never saw in her anything that was not consistent with the character of the saint of Christian chivalry.

The East End

The Law and Liberty League lingered for a year and then expired. The *Link* was extinguished, but before it burnt out it lit up the state

Matchmakers' Union.

THE **QUARTERLY MEETING** of the above Union will take place in ST. LEONARDS ROAD BOARD SCHOOL, on MONDAY, June 16th, at 8.30 p.m.

At a SPECIAL GENERAL MEETING to be held immediately after the conclusion of the Quarterly Meeting, the Secretary will propose that Rule 11 shall be altered to read as follows :—

When the contributions of a Member are four weeks in arrear, he or she shall have notice. When the total arrears owing by a Member reach the amount of a quarter's subscriptions, the name of such Member shall be erased from the Society's books."

Members are earnestly requested to attend the QUARTERLY MEETING, as the question of the reduction of wages at Bell's Factory will be discussed.

ANNIE BESANT,
Hon. Sec.

of things at Messrs. Bryant and May's, and from its articles grew the Match Girls' Strike, which was the precursor of the birth of the New Unionism. There were few workers in London so friendless and helpless as the match girls. The cause seemed hopeless, but Mrs. Besant, with whom was associated in closest comradeship Mr. Herbert Burrows, an old colleague of the Law and Liberty League, and other friends, went down East, supplied the match girls with organisation and courage. They raised funds to maintain the strike ; and ultimately, after a brief but brilliant campaign, achieved a complete victory.

It was that unexpected success, snatched against overwhelming odds by the aid of public sympathy, which rendered possible the Dockers' Strike of 1889, from which the new industrial development of our time may be said to date.

Mrs. Besant's hold upon the East End was very forcibly demonstrated shortly after this by her return as member for the School Board in the largest district in Eastern London. It was a fierce contest, in which one clerical opponent hit below the belt and had to suffer in consequence. It is one of the worst features of Mrs. Besant's absorption in Occultism that it has entailed her retirement from the School Board.

HERBERT BURROWS

V. SPIRITUALISM AND THEOSOPHY

It was about this time that Mrs. Besant, with Mr. Herbert Burrows, began to investigate at regular séances the phenomena of spiritualism. I never attended any of these séances, but heard a good deal about them, especially on one occasion, when the table announced the death of a well-known clergyman, who obligingly mentioned the place of his death, and sent messages to his bereaved relations. Fortunately the table lied, as tables will, for the clergyman shortly after turned up alive and well.

Mrs. Besant was at that time writing reviews occasionally for the *Pall Mall Gazette*. Since the *Link* had died, and the *National Reformer* could not fairly be used in support of Socialism, she had only the *Corner*, a sixpenny monthly, in which to express her views. Madame Blavatsky's *Secret Doctrine* had just appeared, and it was given to Mrs. Besant to review. The reading of that book was the turning point. When I was preparing this article I asked Mrs. Besant to give me briefly the genesis of her Theosophical development. Here is her answer exactly as I received it :

Why Theosophy ?

Could find no answer to problems of life and mind in Materialism, especially as touching—

1. Hypnotic and mesmeric experiments, clairvoyance, etc.
2. Double consciousness, dreams.
3. Effect on the body of mental conceptions.
4. Line between object and subject worlds.
5. Memory, especially as studied in disease.
6. Diseased keenness of sense-perception.
7. Thought transference.
8. Genius, different types of character in family, etc.

These were some of the puzzles. Then Sinnett's books gave me the idea that there might be a different line of investigation possible. I had gone into spiritualism, I went into it again, and got some queer results. But I got no real satisfaction until I got the *Secret Doctrine* from you to review, and then I was all right.

I ought to add that I had long been deeply troubled as to the "beyond" of all my efforts at social and political reform. My own Socialism was that of love, and of levelling up ; there was much Socialism that was of hatred ; and I often wondered if out of hatred any true improvement could spring. I saw that many of the poor were as selfish and as greedy of enjoyment as many of the rich, and sometimes a cold wind of despair swept over me lest the "brute in man" should destroy the realisation of the noblest theories. Here Theosophy, with its proof of the higher nature in man, came as a ray of light, and its teaching of the training of that nature gave solid ground for hope. May I add that its call to limitless self-sacrifice for human good—a call addressed to all who can answer it—came to me as offering satisfaction to what has always been the deepest craving of my nature—the longing to serve as ransom for the race. At once I recognised that here was the path to that which I had been seeking all my life.

It was shortly after that she asked me for an introduction to Madame Blavatsky, which I gladly gave her, little dreaming that I was thereby providing H. P. B. with an heir and successor. Such, however, was the case. Mrs. Besant brought to the Theosophists a zeal and an enthusiasm at least equal to that of H. P. B., while she placed at their service a reputation for absolute sincerity and an eloquence superior to that of any living platform orator. She espoused Madame Blavatsky's cause with the devotion of a neophyte. She sat at her feet learning like a little child all the lore of the Mahatmas; she was obedient in all things;

and when at last Madame Blavatsky passed away, Mrs. Besant was instinctively recognised as her only possible successor.

Materialism Weighed and Found Wanting

When speaking for the last time in the Hall of Science, she said :

You have Materialism of two very different schools. There is the Materialism which cares nothing for man but only for itself. With that Materialism neither I nor those with whom I worked had aught in common. With that Materialism, which is only that of the brute, we never had part nor lot. That is the Materialism that destroys all the glory of human life, it is the Materialism that can only be held by the selfish and, therefore, the degraded. It is never the Materialism that was preached from the platform. Against that Materialism I have no word of reproach to speak now. Never have I spoken word of reproach against it, and I never shall ; for I know that it is a philosophy so selfless in its noblest forms that few are grand enough to grasp it and live it out, and that which I have brought back as fruit from my many years of Materialism is the teaching that, to work without self as the goal is the great object-lesson of human life.

But—and here comes the difference—there are problems in the universe which Materialism not only does not solve but which it declares insoluble—difficulties

ANNIE BESANT
wearing H. P. B.'s ring

in life and mind that Materialism cannot grapple with, and in face of which it is not only dumb, but says that mankind must remain dumb for evermore. Now, in my own studies and my own searching I came upon fact after fact that did not square with the theories of Materialism. I came across facts which were facts of nature as much as any fact of the laboratory or any discovery by the knife or the scapel of the anatomist. Was I to refuse to see them because my philosophy had for them no place? do what men have done in every age—insist that nature was no greater than my knowledge, and that because a fact was new it was, therefore, a fraud or an illusion? Not thus had I learned the lesson of materialistic science from its deepest depths of investigation into nature. And when I found that there were facts that made life other than Materialism deemed; when I found that there were facts of life and consciousness that made the materialistic hypothesis impossible; then I determined still to study, although the foundations were shaking, and not to be recusant enough to the search after truth to draw back because it wore a face other than the one I expected.

The result was the final repudiation of materialism and the adoption of Theosophy.

MADAME BLAVATSKY'S MANTLE

The hubbub that was raised last month about the alleged precipitation of a letter from a

Mahatma, served at least one purpose. It showed that this generation is behind no other that ever existed in thirsting for a sign. To me it is a matter of such supreme indifference whether Koot Hoomi uses the post or materialises his messages on Cashmere paper, that I have not even asked to see any of these much-debated communications. To me the essential miracle is the conversion of Mrs. Besant from Materialism to a firmly based belief in the reality of the spiritual world. We all tried our level best to work that miracle, but we failed. Madame Blavatsky succeeded. Honour where honour is due. To have secured Mrs. Besant for Theosophy is an achievement much more wonderful to me than the duplication of any number of teacups or the tinkling of whole peals of "astral bells."

Mrs. Besant has not only abjured Materialism, she has repudiated her advocacy of neo-Malthusianism. It remains to be seen how long her Socialism will survive. For as she pointed out in a passage of much force and point, Socialism and prudential restraint are indissolubly united.

MALTHUS AND SOCIALISM

Malthus accurately pointed out that population has a tendency to increase beyond the means of subsistence; that as it presses on the available means suffering is caused, and that it is kept within them by what he calls "positive checks," *i.e.*, a high death-rate, especially among the children of the poor, premature death from disease, underfeeding, etc. . . . Unhappily, Malthus added to his scientific exposition some most unfortunate practical advice; he advised the poor not to marry until they had practically reached middle life. The poor felt, with natural indignation, that, in addition to all their other deprivations, they were summoned by Malthus to give up the chief of the pleasures left to them, to surrender marriage, to live a joyless celibacy through the passion season of life, to crush out all the impulses of love until by long repression these would be practically destroyed. . . . The shocking prostitution, which is the curse of every Christian city, is the result of the following of the advice of Malthus so far as marriage is concerned. It is obvious that Malthus ignored the strength of the sexual instinct, and that the only possible result of the wide acceptance of his teaching would be the increase of prostitution, an evil more terrible than that of poverty. But the objection rightly raised to the teaching of Malthus ought not to take the form of assailing the perfectly impregnable law of population, nor is it valid against the teachings of neo-Malthusians, who advise early marriage, and limitation of the family within the means. The acceptance of this doctrine is absolutely essential to the success of Socialism. I have not yet heard any answer to this which bears even a plausible semblance of real cogency.

Her Present Position

This, however, is but a side issue. The great and startling phenomenon which we have to consider is the fact that the Soul of the Materialist platform has now become the high priestess of a system of spiritual philosophy which is substantially Christian in ethics, and which in many points seems to supply a scientific foundation for much that has been most cavilled at in the Christian creeds. Mrs. Besant has not yet reached her ultimate development. She has her loins girt up and is in readiness to follow wherever Truth may lead. Not hers as yet is the sublime certainty of the love of the Almighty Father. But she is no longer left comfortless. She may not have realised the Fatherhood of God, but she has entered into a realising sense of the communion of the saints. Christ may only be to her a Mahatma of the first rank. He is at least more real and brother-like to her to-day than He has ever been, not even excepting the early days when she pored over "The Fathers of the Church" and decorated the mission chapel for Eastertide. She has been led by a strange road, as were the Children of Israel in their forty years in the wilderness, but the pillar of cloud by day and the pillar of fire by night fail not, nor fails her readiness to follow wheresoever they may lead.

For her, and for all who, like her, have their faces turned *Zionward*, ever wandering in the outer darkness, arises unceasing from the unconscious soul that yearns ever for closer union with its God, the prayer of which Newman, more clearly than other mortals, caught some far-away echoes in his familiar hymn :

Lead, kindly Light, amid the encircling gloom,
Lead Thou me on :
The night is dark, and I am far from home,
Lead Thou me on :
Keep Thou my feet ; I do not ask to see
The distant scene ; one step enough for me.

I was not ever thus, nor prayed that Thou
Shouldst lead me on ;
I loved to choose and see my path, but now
Lead Thou me on.
I loved the garish day, and, spite of fears,
Pride ruled my will : remember not past years.

So long Thy power hath blessed me, sure it still
Will lead me on
O'er moor and fen, o'er crag and torrent, till
The night is gone.
And with the morn those angel faces smile
Which I have loved long since, and lost awhile.

THEOSOPHY AND CHRISTIANITY

What Theosophy is to Mrs. Besant she has told us in the letter which she addressed to the *Daily Chronicle* last month, from which we can form some idea of the spiritual nutriment which she extracts from the somewhat misty, mystical system which is the natural child of the marriage of Christianity and Buddhism. In a world where the best men and women of the loftiest and most orthodox creeds are often driven to cry in the anguish of their hearts for a closer and more vivid realisation of the Inner Presence, or for anything which would be for their soul's good, it is not for us, or for any one, to criticise unkindly the teaching which to any fellow-being has made the world anew and restored the soul to mankind. But while gratefully recognising Madame Blavatsky as an instrument in bringing Mrs. Besant from the outer darkness into the brotherhood of those who believe in the spiritual as opposed to the material, to the soul as opposed to the body, there is to me something lacking in Theosophy. There is no note which vibrates more constantly in the soul of every true man—and the truer he is the more it vibrates—than the prayer of the publican, " Lord, be merciful to me, a sinner ! " That despairing cry rises from the deepest and innermost recesses of our being. It finds an answer in the story of the Woman taken in adultery, in the parable of the Prodigal, in the death of the Crucified. To that heartfelt cry I do not find an answer in Theosophy. I find, on the contrary, an almost exultant assertion of the opposing doctrines, that God is not a Being with a father's heart, that for sin there is no expiation, and for the sinner no forgiveness. There is much fascination about the Theosophical philosophy, much, I believe, that is true in many of its apparently fantastic teachings ; but it would indeed be an Aladdin's choice of new lamps for old, if for this we were to abandon that faith in the Fatherhood of God which Jesus lived and died to impart to mankind. But although Theosophy may to our deepest consciousness be a very unsatisfying thing compared with the living faith in the Fatherhood of God, the Brotherhood of Christ, and the Motherhood of the Church that is inspired by the Holy Spirit, still do not let us ignore the fact that it is immeasurably nearer Christianity than the barren blank materialistic negation from which it has been a stepping-stone for Mrs. Besant's escape. Theosophist she may remain to the end of her life ; but if so, then it is Theosophy which will bring her nearer still to the living and loving heart of God.

"You are so good," said her favourite aunt the last time she saw her on earth ; "any one so good as you must come to our dear Lord at last."

Printed in the United States
124457LV00004B/122/A

9 781417 976867